AF471760

Visible & Physical Manifestation of Spirits
A look from inside the Grimoires

By Tolka Scrolls

ISBN:978-1-4717-0282-2

Disclaimer and Terms of Use:

The Author and Publisher has striven to be as accurate and complete as possible in the creation of this book.. While all attempts have been made to verify information provided in this publication, the Author and Publisher assumes no responsibility for errors, omissions, or contrary interpretation of the subject matter herein. Any perceived slights of specific persons, peoples, or organizations are unintentional. In practical advice books, like anything else in life, there are no guarantees. Readers are cautioned to rely on their own judgment about their individual circumstances and to act accordingly. All links are for information purposes only and are not warranted for content, accuracy or any other implied or explicit purpose.

Table of Contents

Introduction

This book is for the practicing, or aspiring magician, in regards to learning about the appearance of spirits in the grimoires and thus will be of particular interest to Ceremonial Magicians. However is not really exclusive to them and would be useful to anyone who has not yet seen a spirit visibly.

I first started magic in October 2001, but was by no means foreign to the concept of the spirit world. I had focused mostly on personal powers, by which I mean telepathy, telekinesis, and other forms of magic that did not require a spirits presence. Although I had minor success at time I was not greatly successful with any of these, despite being raised to follow this path by my father who was very good at this kind of magic, and in October/November 2001 I decided I would try calling on the aid of outside help instead. I guess this is what most people would call magic, or if you are new age and really like to put k's on things for no reason: magick.

I got some candles some books and set to work my first invocation. It wasn't particularly well done, but it was I guess very Ceremonial. I had seen shadows before I started this type of magic which I believe had been attracted by my previous efforts with personal powers, but the first time I can remember seeing a spirit in magic proper was a person made of fire coming through the wall towards the little candle I had in the circle, the candle then went out at his presence and he left, it was also the first time a result actually followed. I was pretty terrified to be honest; it was hardly the timid shadows I had seen out of the corner of my eye, or passing quickly, this was a very confident man made of pure fire and I can't say you ever get used to seeing something like that full on, but you do at least learn to expect it.

From then on when I practiced my magic they turned up I saw them and the results followed, but if I did something wrong and they didn't turn up (I didn't see them) then the results didn't follow. It was pretty simple going, as long as I could get things right for them to turn up everything would go smoothly despite them clearly detesting me.

I had it in my head at the time there were witches and the like everywhere summoning spirits but keeping quiet about it, although I didn't know any others it made sense with all of these books out there enabling people. At the time I was using a mix of Ceremonial Magic unbeknown to me, Romany Gypsy and Witchcraft and had not decided particularly on any path then, so everyone who practiced any type of magic I figured probably had great power. To be honest with you I was only interested in taking what worked and was true out of each. I had been raised to think scientifically and that was the way I wanted to go in to magic. After a few years I settled into a type of magic called Ceremonial Magic, purely by accident. I would like to stress here although I should not need to, that when I say Ceremonial Magic I am talking about grimoire magic, as in what is written in the grimoires, a series of magical instruction manuals written in the medieval period and practiced by Christians and Jews, not lodge magic organizations like the OTO,

Golden Dawn etc. Although originally I had used some Lodge Magic ceremonies much as from other paths; as I experimented with what I could drop and what I needed I had dropped all of theirs for being thoroughly useless. I ended up with a pretty set system, still I thought quite mixed and I wanted to expand it a little. In 2006 I delved deeper in to some of the symbols that I was using and their origins and found that they were Ceremonial Magic from grimoires, in fact it turned out that my only mixing was from one grimoire to the next, by that point I had dropped pretty much everything but what was mentioned in the grimoires without realizing that Ceremonial Magic existed as something in itself and that there were grimoires. I merely had a collection of parts from books. Some magic I hadn't dropped because it did not work, Witchcraft and Romany Gypsy magic I had dropped merely because it wasn't as powerful and I didn't visibly see spirits with it when I used it which seemed to be a defining feature of larger success. I am fully open to the idea that there are many types of magic which work.

It was 2009 before I stumbled on other magicians and I talked to them with a great deal of eagerness, although I found some of their opinions on spirits didn't quite sit easy with what I had seen I was ecstatic to find others who knew that magic was real. I even began to speak to modern day writers on the occult, but again I found they seemed a little off in what they thought, just the odd thing they would say would nag at me and I would think, 'how can you think that if you've ever had contact?' but I disregarded these things at the time. I didn't particularly want to make argument over small issues.

Visible & Physical Manifestation of Spirits

A look from inside the Grimoires

I guess it was a few months before the appearance of spirits come into conversation and it was then that the proverbial penny dropped that most of them had never seen a spirit. Further I found that those that said they had, clearly were talking rubbish. Even results which happened to me with a three days usually to a week, was a time frame they were unaccustomed to, passing off coincidences sometimes six months down the line as a result of a spell. Quite honestly I was shocked. I had unfortunately assumed that most people had put in the effort until they had got a spirit turn up like it states you are to do in the book, but I quickly came to the realization that their odd ways of thinking were actually because they had never summoned anything, but their own imaginations.

Then as I delved deeper I found an underground of misinformation circling the internet to cover it. I was told that when you see spirits they are visions, or hallucinations, or perhaps you are asleep. I was told that you can only see spirits in mirrors, or by putting yourself in an altered state or drugs, and often I was told that the grimoires reflected these ideas. None of this sat right with me considering my experiences and I had some 8 years of it already at that point. I had read as many grimoires as I could get my hands on and also failed to see how the grimoires supported these notions. To make it clear I don't take drugs, never have, neither have I put myself in an altered state when I have seen spirits, neither does it put you in an altered state when you do see them, unless by altered state you mean fear. In fact they used to turn up hours later than I called and it was years before I came up with the system they were using to time their visits on and learned to know when to expect them. I was hardly sat there meditating into a mirror. It was absolutely crazy to me that I was suddenly in a world with hundreds of other magicians who were doing the same rituals and getting no visible appearance and further that none of them believed that I could.

Somehow I become known as the guy who had 'physical manifestation.' which is a term used by a writer called Lisiewski for something similar to what I have seen. His views dodn't sit that well with me either, but I am happy enough at least he doesn't believe that spirits are visions. Through supporters of his I managed to find others who also had seen spirits, fall into groups of serious magicians and I realized that those who have physically seen a spirit are there, they were actually just a well hidden minority of the occult circuit.

Now you would think that they wouldn't be well hidden if they are the serious practitioners, but I soon found out why they were. One thing you don't realize when you get appearance of a physical spirit, is that if you mention it you will enrage anyone who hasn't. I have been repeatedly threatened by management of occult forums for defending my position, had my account hacked and even had my posts altered by moderators on two separate forums likely many times before I noticed it was happening. My email was also hacked and each time these happened after getting involved in arguments where I was told that spirits can't appear outright and that I am lying.

So finally I have decided to write a book about physical manifestation or visible appearance or whatever you want to call it, and clean up some of those nasty true lies that circulate so freely. With information comes power and I hope that with this book more people will understand how spirits actually appear, what the appearance is, and what legitimate ways of seeing them there are. Tips for aiding the appearance of a physical spirit are also mentioned as I go through it all, and summed up at the end. I'm not going to give you a long drawn out explanation of my opinions based on my practical work using the grimoires, most of you won't believe it and have bought this book out of interest or in an attempt to debunk it, and those that do believe in physical visible manifestation are more interested in getting it for themselves, so I will save you from my drivel. However, some practical experience that I have had kind of ties the gap between a few viewpoints so I will insert my opinions into your tender side like a sharp sword here and there. Mostly this book concerns the actual grimoire accounts of the subject, straight from the medieval wizards mouth. I have tried to use source texts rather than the later mixes of them when I can.

CHAPTER ONE

What is Visible Physical Manifestation of a spirit?

There is such a division in opinion in modern times over whether a spirit becomes physical like us, how it does it, or if it merely just a vision. The 'it's all a vision' concept is propelled by many authors out there today who refuse to actually read any grimoire that they talk about. Yet the answers are already there and written down. On the other side of the coin there seem to be people who are convinced that spirits alter their state to become flesh and blood, to be scientifically like living things and are discomforted by this. I would disagree with this point also.

The term Physical Manifestation is from one particularly writer, but I would like to talk about it on a much broader scale of the definition of the words themselves as physical manifestation is commonly used to simply mean a visible physical spirit.

In my view visible physical manifestation does not mean solid. More to the point physical does not mean solid either. I need to stress this point!

Physical Visible Manifestation of a spirit means that the spirit is legitimately there, as in actually physically there and seeable, not that it has a solid form that you can touch.

Some of the spirits appear as fire, some as lght. These guys aren't solid like flesh and blood. They don't have veins and blood pumping through them, but they are physically manifested as what they are supposed to be either fire or light. Some have basically no form and move more like wind, but again these are already written in the grimoires. So if we are going to base our views on the grimoires then we need to accept that visible physical manifestation doesn't at any point mean that they suddenly change their form and become something scientific. If they want to be a man made of fire, they can be. That fire can be real, don't be thinking that it can't, but there needs to be no reason for it to be there in the form of a human or whatever else other than the spirit whose taken it as a body wants it to be, neither does that fire become capable of burning things unless they want it to. These guys are still outside of science, or at least outside of what we commonly accept as science today and it is important to keep that in mind.

This book will help you understand what visible manifestation is, how it works, and how to achieve it by looking at the grimoires themselves so that you can understand their concepts of spirits bodies.

I need to address another point first too and that is that visible and solid aren't the same thing either. If you see something which is actually there, it does not have to be solid. Bare with me if this seems obvious to you and needless for me to bring up, but this seems a really hard concept for some people to grasp and seems to be a base for some of their wild theories. I will give an example where visible and solid are not the same thing, which you should be able to accept.

Infrared light is a spectrum of electromagnetic wave which gives off heat and is outside of the visible spectrum frequencies and guess what it exists. I know it's mind blowing isn't it. You can stick your hand right through it but yet it is real. Something which is legitimate and yet isn't solid. In fact you can also get some pretty cool equipment which allows you to see that if you should wish to. So hopefully I have established something does not have to be visible and solid to exist for you. Even when you are looking at it through special cameras you can still put your hand through it, because visible does not mean it has to be solid to exist.

Now here is a thought; what about if infra-red were conscious? I'm not saying it is, just giving a what if scenario to pass over a point so please don't quote this out of context.

Imagine for a moment that Mr. Infra-Red could make himself visible or not, he just is not choosing to most of the time. I mean electromagnetism is also visible light, it's just the frequency that changes it's visibility, so let's just say that as electromagnetism Mr. Infra-Red could shift it from the infra-red frequency to visible light frequency and bam he is visible. In fact just for a moment let's say that he doesn't even have to have physical effects like heat unless he wants to, because that of course is another effect of a specific frequency. I don't believe that spirits are electromagnetic frequencies and I want to make that clear, but I do believe they are much the same as this example. A spirit can be come visible, does actually exist, and yet doesn't have to be solid. Really we need to entirely separate the idea that something visible means something solid, or else it's a vision, because this is just not true. A vision implies that it is not real, you are seeing something which is false, something made by a spirit but of no physical properties itself, something which is purely illegitimate. A vision implies that it is less than Mr. Infra-Red, that there is nothing there at all, however the unphysical spirit can cause you to hallucinate an image to communicate with if it wants to.

Of course there is little to no evidence to support this vision claim in the grimoires. It is largely made by people who have simply never really seen a spirit and are trying to cover their failures. On the other hand spirits that are simply not solid are more than viable in the grimoires and this is why I often fall out with both sides of the great divide.

Spirits do have a real form it's not just a thought, a spirit has some type of body too, be it an ethereal body or whatever you want to call it and the reasons for thinking this from the grimoires will be discussed later, so the idea that spirits are visions is rubbish in my opinion. When you see the spirit, it actually is the spirit.

Now you are probably thinking from this that I am also rubbishing the opinion that spirits can be physically solid right? Not at all. I do firmly believe that they can become solid. Of course they 'can be'. They just don't have to be to appear and this is what I am trying to make clear first. If you want him to manifest as physical brick then when you put your hand on him, he is as solid as brick is. All I will say is that this is separate to being visible. A spirit can become visible and a spirit can become solid, but these do not have to be at the same time.

CHAPTER TWO

Visible Manifestation of a spirit in the actual grimoires

Classifications of Physical appearance are easy to come across in the grimoires. Probably the most controversial texts for this is the Heptameron. A lot of people see that it is saying that spirits are not physical but visions, however the Heptameron in fact explains clearly enough that a vision and a spirit manifesting are two completely different things. I am going to address this particular grimoire first because of it's common use in arguments.

After attempting to summon the spirits with conjurations in the ritual, it states:

"These things being duly performed, there will appear infinite visions, apparitions, phantasms" - Heptameron.

Okay, so you are looking at this and thinking 'what the hell!' that is saying that spirits are visions; you are conjuring then visions turn up. If you believe in physical manifestation you may have just had a nasty sinking feeling in your gut. Well, I will continue this quote and go in to it in more depth to understand what it means, but for now I would like to address this particular part as I have seen it used in a number of arguments to say that spirits are visions and not ever physical. I really want to drum that in to your heads. In fact I have been quoted this exactly and you will see what deception has gone in to it by not including any more of the paragraph.

So often left out by vision propagators, this is the end of that particular piece:

"You shall see an infinite company of archers, with a great multitude of horrible beasts, which will arrange themselves as if they would devour the companions; nevertheless, fear nothing. Then the exorcist holding the pentacle in his hand, let him say; 'Avoid hence these iniquities, by virtue of the banner of God.' Then will the spirits be compelled to obey the exorcist, and the company shall see them no more."

If you didn't catch that. The exorcist just told the spirits he is calling to behave and get rid of the visions which were made false by them. Have a problem with that? Of course you do, it is terribly written, and so I will explain. Your problem, no doubt: "Then will the spirits be compelled to obey the exorcist, and the company shall see them no more." suggests that it is referring to the visions as spirits and you tell them to go away. In fact it isn't. The visions are made by the spirits you are calling, and it is them that the passage is referring to.

It would be clearer if it read "Then will the spirits you have been pure for nine days, fasted for three days and whose name you have written out and just attempted to conjure, be compelled to obey the exorcist, and the company shall see the visions no more." but you know, they expected some common sense and they were terrible writers. A bit like me, but medieval. You're not convinced? Well that's why I've written more about it.

Firstly reaffirming why the visions were made by the spirits you are calling; "These things being duly performed, there will appear infinite visions, apparitions, phantasms, beating of drums, and the sound of all kinds of musical instruments, which is done by the spirits, that with the terror they might force some of the companions out of the circle." Yes that's the same as before but I've had the courtesy to include more of that quote. So basically the spirits are making some visions to scare you out of the circle. Note here that it is saying that the spirits are making the visions, and not that the spirits are the visions. Read it again. It's pretty clear. Sadly this part is usually cut off when quoted. At no point can you suggest that it means musical instruments are the only thing the spirits are doing to strike terror in to the companions, quite simply put, they just aren't that scary and it is referring to that specific part before it continues on. So at this point I guess you can see why the whole thing is rarely quoted in arguments. It is merely meant to read "Spirits make things that aren't real to scare your companions out of the circle. You tell them to behave. They stop."

But okay so we have established visions appeared when he was trying to call the spirits to scare the companions out of the circle, this is undeniable, it's written in the grimoire itself, and you are half convinced that they themselves weren't spirits, but it still doesn't say that the spirits themselves once they appear aren't visions as well does it?

Well aside from the fact if they were the spirits you would have achieved your goal and not be sending them away, I mean if the visions were the spirits and it was talking about them then it is stating you have control of the vision spirits. "Then will the spirits be compelled to obey the exorcist," it seems a bit silly to send them away? and the fact spirits made the visions, it kind of does imply they weren't spirits at all. Even if you say the army was legitimate spirits it still remains the spirits make the visions and thus aren't them. I see no way you can twist it any other way.

After the visions are gone you continue to call the spirit to your presence as you want it specifically by the circle and to appear.

"Then they will immediately come in their proper forms; and when you see them before the circle, show them the pentacle." etc.

I think that's pretty clear. Now you have actually got the spirits to turn up. It states here also in their proper form, but those of you on the physical manifestation side need not wet your pants in excitement too much either about this as there is more to it.

You see you asked them to come in a peaceable form and what it's talking about here is that they are coming 'see-able' but not how you want them, perhaps in a grotesque appearance or perhaps this indicates a spiritual body.

After continuing to tell them your balls are made of Christ's biceps and other such things to scare them it states "suddenly they will appear in a peaceable form"

You can then give them the warmest welcome "Wherefore, I bind you, that you remain affable and visible before this circle" and abracademy you have yourself a bound spirit.

Which brings us to the segment I want to point out. "you remain affable and visible" where it states that it is them being visible, not having no form and making you have a vision. "you remain ' ' visible" Read it again until it sinks in.

But really the Heptameron is the least of your problems if you are attempting to promote that there isn't such a thing as a spirit appearing without it being a vision, because there are a lot of other grimoires that explain it much clearer, and even how the spirits do it. I doubt that you are that convinced just yet by this alone, I just wanted to explain what the Heptameron is talking about as it is so often misquoted by vision propagators.

CHAPTER THREE

Are spirits forms set or changeable?

You may have noticed that in the Heptameron they come in a different form to what you make them change in to. Again this is reflected in many grimoires, the Key of Solomon also has in the conjurations instructions to come in peaceable forms and not hideous or deformed. This means that whether they can become physical or not, what physical body they choose is in someway up to them and not set, and that you also have some control over it. Now divisions of spirits in my research may behave in different ways on this subject.

In the Sepher Raziel it explains very clearly a spirit taking a body. I would also like to point out that the Heptameron is largely based on the Sepher Raziel and the later Liber Juratus.

"A signe ascendent sheweth the body. The Lord of the Ascendent or the planet that is in the ascendent or which beholdeth it sheweth it his spirit. And the Lord of the houre signifieth his soule & his will."

If you are not an astrologer this probably means nothing to you. That's fine. I will explain it anyway.

During a day, the Sun goes around the Earth (from the perspective of someone on the Earth) So it rises and sets, then seems to go underneath us where it pops back up roughly where it was before. Happy Sunrise! Well the Sun is in a tropical zodiac constellation for around a month, so actually as the sun goes around us, so does the sign it's in with it and yes the whole zodiac. It's like an ever turning ring around us, some signs rising up on the horizon, some above us, some signs setting on the horizon like the sun does, and some traveling out of view where we can't see them underneath. They are all around us and the Sun stays in whatever sign is relevant to that month and travels around us with the zodiac ring. You may be dubious of this because you don't see the stars until night time, but that's because the sun is so bright, they are all there all the time going around us, the sun light just stops you seeing them. It's because of light pollution, similar to you not being able to see your phone screen in the bright sunlight.

I will break down the relevant information now that you understand that. "A signe ascendent sheweth the body." means literally, that whatever sign is rising on the horizon at the time the spirit turns up will show (be similar to/ represent) the body the spirit manifests with. Ie. If it's Gemini it may be two headed, or appear as twins. Why? Because Gemini is the sign of the twins and that's just the kind of thing those funky little twins like to do.

This is by no means a foreign idea. In Natal Astrology this is much similar for people. Often we say that when a person is born with the Sun in a certain sign, they have certain visible characteristics, Scorpio's and Aries tend to have brown eyes. etc. Well the sign rising on the horizon when you were born also affects the way that you look in Astrology. So the Sepher Raziel is saying that as it is true for humans so also is it true for spirits. When you summon a spirit, he makes a body relevant to what is on the horizon, though much more dramatically like it because he doesn't have to stick to the basic human design.

The Grimorium Verum also 'may' agree with this, and in my opinion probably does, but I will quote it and you can decide. It states: "Spirits do not always appear in the same shape. This is because they are not themselves of matter or form, and have to find a body to appear in, and one suitable to their intended manifestation and appearance." I believe again this is talking about finding the body from the ascendant as in the earlier Sepher Raziel grimoire. Many of the later grimoires were trying to appear less complex and the magicians much more intelligent. They grazed over the whys of something and it left them some mystery. They were the guy who could tell you how to do things, but they were the ones who knew why it worked and that was staying with them.

Okay, that's all well and good, but if spirits manifesting are influenced the same as new born babies by astrology, then if we also look different due to where the sun is (our Sun/Zodiac Sign), surely that should also have some impact on the spirit's look as well?

To answer this I will direct you to the Goetia. This can be read two ways, so I will let you decide:

"...a great president and appereth in Sagittarius that is his shape when ye Sun is there" this is written under his seal. No description of his appearance is given. So what is his shape when the Sun is in Sagittarius? His seal? he looks like a squiggle? or does it mean that he looks a bit Centaur like (Sagittarius) when the Sun is there.

Again this simply follows how Astrology works for people. Your looks are effected by the Sun's position, and the sign on the ascendant, and so are theirs. It is just the same for them. It's like each time you call them to appear, they are influenced like a new born baby with the characteristics of those main astrological points.

Now you maybe thinking there is more to us than just that. What about genetics? If both our parents have blonde hair and brown eyes, it's unlikely that we will be born with black hair and blue eyes. Is there perhaps also something like this which affects spirits?

We are all on Earth, and being affected by the planets around us, all of which have certain attributes which are affecting us. Spirits of a planetary nature on the other hand, are generally just affected by that one planets attributes, thus will also have characteristics of their planet dominate over them. So yes, the appearance of a spirit is three-fold, ascendant, sun, and if you like a type of planetary genetics. So this means that if you want him to appear as a woman with blonde hair and blue eyes, you are better to do it with a spirit of Venus, with the Sun and Venus in Libra and ascending. Libra - blonde hair blue eyes, Venus - woman. Often people ask for the wrong type of body from a spirit which makes it much more difficult, or should I say perhaps ask at the wrong times. Take in mind what the Grimorium Verum says again: "Spirits do not always appear in the same shape. ' and have to find a body to appear in, and one suitable to their intended manifestation and appearance." Make it easier for them you will get appearance easier, make it harder for them, and you are making it harder for yourself.

There are a list of common appearances in Agrippa's Fourth Book of Occult Philosophy which may fit what I was referring to earlier as planetary genetics, ie. basic forms that spirits of planets tend to try and take. I haven't found them incredibly accurate in practice, but again I do think they should be taken in to account if you are telling a spirit to appear a certain way. There are similar descriptions of planetary spirits in the Liber Juratus which could also be used as a guide.

CHAPTER FOUR

So what are spirits bodies?

Okay, now this is a real hard one to answer. The simple fact is there are many contradictions and no one knows which is real. Some would say that a spirit is physical but invisible, but like quoted above the grimoires on the whole wouldn't agree. We know that the appearance of the spirit can not only be altered by itself but by the time that it is called. This is acceptable even for die hard traditionalists, (whatever they are,) as it is in the grimoires.

Others would say that they have no body at all, and take one on. This is acceptable from the religious point of view as well. That a spirit has no real body. However, it does say in the bible that God made us in his image, so we have to tread carefully among the die hard Christians and Jews and others of similar religious backgrounds.

Others say they never have a body and cause you to have a vision. This is wrong according to most grimoires and already been addressed but it will be further shown as false as this continues.

It seems looking at the grimoires on the whole a spirit is just a spirit. He doesn't really have any set form until you tell him to, then that is influenced by said things. Yet, there must be an essence there to take the form in the first place. It does seem that even before you tell a spirit to appear a certain way you are calling him to the circle. So for one thing it suggests he isn't everywhere, he isn't what they call Omnipresent, instead he moves about the universe wherever he is allowed/likes, otherwise there wouldn't be anything to call before the circle or command into a triangle. You can also see this in the conjurations where you call a spirit to your circle from one place or another, pretty much trying to cover every place he could be hiding other than under your bed or in that creepy old closet that came with the house. So spirits do have some 'form' at all times. Even if that form maybe formless, like a focal point of a much wider consciousness, it's really there as something, but not perhaps with a definition in terms of how we would think of something until it takes a body.

Taking this in mind and how a spirit appears, we see when we are telling the spirit to come before us and appear, we are telling this essence to come to us and appear in the way it naturally does, as already discussed, and in a way bordering on not terrifying. After all, the last thing you need after collecting all your equipment is soiled holy garments. But again you are calling him to manifest.

So this essence, seems unexplainable, but a few grimoires seem to give their opinions on it nonetheless:

"Some are created from water. Others from wind, unto which they are like. Some from earth. Some from clouds. Others from solar vapors. Others from the keenness and strength of fire; and when they are invoked or summoned, they come always with great noise, and with the terrible nature of fire." - The Greater Key of Solomon. Mathers.

So you could say before manifestation they are made by an element, or a few elements, by which I mean Fire, Earth, Air and Water, or you could say that too is merely part of them taking some form which they don't naturally have. And even if the essence of a spirit is elemental in some nature or cosmic does that mean physical or does that mean a spiritual version of it. Simple fact is, it is impossible to say. Another thing that is evident in the Greater Key is that there are different types of spirits. Those it mentions don't seem to be those that actually fit those in the pentacles later given. If there are many types perhaps it is impossible to say for certain how spirits exist and appear, perhaps it is different depending on the type and that we can truly only talk about those in the grimoires in general which are 'usually' planetary.

Another problem when we start talking about particular types of spirits is that the opinion in the grimoires varies much more wildly. For example concerning those made by the solar vapors

The Greater Key continues: "When the spirits which are created from the vapors of the Sun are invoked, they come under a very beautiful and excellent form, but filled with pride, vanity, and conceit. "

If you notice earlier it mentions these separate to those of fire, and goes on to say that those made of solar vapors appear with jewelery (decoration) and vainglory in the way they dress. Whereas in the Liber Juratus it states:

"And they do reign in the spheres of the stars, and they do take upon them a firey body when they be sent by the commandment of God to man in this world that be cleansed and purified to company with them, and to comfort them. And of them there are seven sorts whose natures ought to be known, "

When it says stars it is talking about the five traditional planets here and the Sun and Moon, but the idea the angels appear as fire people is pretty much the idea portrayed throughout all of them, nonetheless for the Sun in particular: "Their bodies are long and slender, pale or yellow, and their region is the North."

Interestingly those under the angels of the Sun are much different, but would not be formed from the vapors of the Sun itself so I'm not sure whether that is who the Greater Key may be referring to or not.

CHAPTER FIVE
Solidity in the Grimoires

So nowadays we have a lot of stories about people summoning spirits in their bedroom having some feelings and five years later something happens and of course it must be a result which proves their experiences to be real. This is all well and good if you want to believe this, but in reality spirits are extremely dangerous things. I once had my window ripped off its hinges by a spirit who was angry. I have also had them knock doors open and move things out of the way, and these were still invisible. So before I go into the grimoires I would again like to make my opinion clear that a spirit can take a form, make it solid, or remain out of phase so that things can move through it, or a spirit can make a body and turn that solid enough to do things. Solidity and visibility are two separate things not dependent on each other.

The Key of Knowledge which predates most versions of the Key of Solomon and is a christian version. It is more than likely closer to the original than say the Hygromentea in my opinion. It is interesting in many respects as it words things slightly differently to most of the others and the appearance of spirits is no different. In the Key of Solomon/Knowledge you are usually to make a candle which will help make the spirits appear. It states specifically in the Key of Knowledge as you command the candle fire: "that thou light the spirits which will appear here."

Note that it is saying that you have made a candle to 'light up' the spirits that may try and remain invisible, in fact the idea that spirits may remain invisible isn't foreign to the Key of Solomon genre at all, there is also a Sun Pentacle for making spirits appear who don't want to. For good reason as there are many accounts of what happens if they get you unaware. "It is recorded in several of the ancient British authors, that Peters, the celebrated magician of Devonshire, together with his associates, having exorcised one of these malicious spirits to conduct them to a subterranean vault, where a considerable quantity of treasure was known to be hid, they had no sooner quit the magic circle, than they were instantaneously crushed into atoms, as it were in the twinkling of an eye." - A New and Complete Illustration of the Occult Sciences, Book 4. Sibly. So a spirit that is not visible can still be as solid as if it were. Again this does show that visibility and solidity are not hand in hand.

You could argue that it takes a body from the astrological places required as before mentioned when you call it, and from then you have to make it appear, or you could argue that this is before it takes the body at all and its natural form has substance too. It is a mute point as there is no clear concise grimoire answer. I could give you my opinion but what's that worth when you have one too. There is however, overwhelming support that a spirit can become solid enough to knock the holy water, tears and sweat from your sweet face.

There are other accounts as well of course. For example asking a spirit to put its hand on a book and swear its allegiance. Never-mind the various places where a spirit can give you things or indeed build things for you, which is lets face it, pretty hard for a vision. Often these are just promises of which may just be what the spirit in question has told the magician it can do, without actually doing it. However some greater thought is sometimes included which suggests also practical experience of this. In the Little Black Book of Venus for example it explains that you have to take whatever the spirit gives you and transfer it into a separate box other than the one he has given it to you in. This to me suggests a magician working around possible foul play on the spirits part. It also seems unlikely that no one who asks spirits what they could do and had them fully constrained ever just asked them to actually do it, so there is no reason to really doubt the grimoire writing magician's word on what the spirits can do, especially as he is telling you how to summon the spirit yourself.

The doubt which has arisen is really due to lack of success. It's a bit like someone saying they don't believe in pick up lines because the people they've tried them on didn't respond.

CHAPTER SIX

Power over spirits who are physically there

One of the differences I have with some of the other propagators of spirits being able to take a physical solid form is that I don't believe it allows any more power over a spirit whereas most of them have got the idea it does. Neither do I see any evidence in the grimoires that a spirit manifested is forced to obey you simply for this reason. It seems to me largely you are asking it to appear purely to know where he is. If you had complete control of a spirit you could do some wonderful things. I haven't seen anyone doing this. Although I have had some great success, I have not won the lottery and become a millionaire and as far as I am aware neither has anyone else who practices. I have 'some' control, but that control is a variable, I do not accept that you have control completely at any point, they will always be somewhat resilient and it is always a battle to get them to agree to what you ask.

What I will say however, is that it is a sign of control, rather than a method of it. If you can't get it to appear, it's unlikely that you are going to be able to get it to do anything else, so I take those who can see spirits more seriously than those who don't.

CHAPTER SEVEN

But what about Visions as opposed to actual physical appearance?

Despite me and the grimoires being wholly against spirits being visions, or hallucinations caused by spirits, it is unacceptable for me to say that spirits cannot cause visions if they want to. As we see in the Heptameron they can very well make you see things. This is of course different to you lighting them up with a magic candle this is them making something purely illegitimate to trick you.

On the other-hand visions aren't just used to trick, they can also be used to teach. I myself have been shown visions by actual spirits to explain things to me. There is a pentacle of Jupiter which gives visions, in the Magical Calendar there is a table for visions. In the Liber Juratus there is a rite to see a vision of the Lord God. Visions can often help you see things which are otherwise hard to show you, landscapes, symbols and the like. All I will say is that if you don't have control of the spirit to make it appear it is unlikely that you have control to make it show you visions either. Spirits are real, their bodies are made by astrological science, their form is solid or not depending on their will, their visibility is a matter of choice unless you have control over them, but visions as completely separate things which these spirits make are also legitimately written in the grimoires and should not be discarded. It is just important to remember that they clearly are separate things to the appearance of the spirit you are calling, not the same. Which brings me to the next chapter nicely.

CHAPTER EIGHT

Mirrors, Crystals and Dream invocations

Mirrors, Crystals and Dream invocations are all perfectly legitimate methods that have been used in the grimoires and modernly. However, some of their purposes have been twisted to fit modern views rather than what they are meant for and so I will go over them here. Firstly I will discuss mirrors very briefly. In one of the base Grimoires of the Solomonic cycle (although not Solomonic itself) the Sepher Raziel it states that you can ordain yourself with the juice of Cannabis and Arthemesy, before a steel mirror, and that it will give you the power to see spirits and other abilities, but the point is that the mirror is legitimate in the grimoire tradition as it is mentioned in one of the source texts of later works. Now the use of drugs here which should never be followed without checking local laws and indeed health risks (some highly poisonous things are sometimes suggested) are common in that grimoire. A grimoire that is amusingly one of the oldest with reference of non-physical appearance of spirits.

Another thing which is talked about a lot by magicians are magic crystals. I would like to explain that traditionally crystals were not for people who could not make spirits appear normally, as is pushed by the many occultists who use them today, insisting physical appearance outside of something is impossible. No, in fact crystals were used the same as the triangle of art, or the brass vase in the Lesser Key of Solomon, they were used to bind the spirits so that you had their obedience. The basic idea was that light was holy, and that spirits being holy therefore behaved like light. As light was trapped in crystals and the like, so then could spirits be trapped, and that is exactly what they are: spirit traps. This did however (as illogical as it may be) often also include trapping bad spirits in as well. In fact the use of crystals far predates the grimoires and any understanding they had on it. Often the trapped spirits were incarcerated in rings and used for set purposes the magician that wore it wanted them for and especially depending on the type of crystal and its power of this there were often bindings to keep them trapped. The crystal itself was seen as an aid.

In the grimoire's use of crystals this was similarly done and many times also as a useful medium to give visions in the crystal. The visions are described as things outside of the spirit for example places of treasure, people far away etc that you want to observe. Note however that you are telling the spirit in these cases to cause the visions, and they are not the visions themselves.

Another Interesting observance in the grimoires is that it often focused on certain types of spirits. A defining feature is either that the spirits are people's souls, or that usually that they have a direction and an earthly assignment, King, Prince etc.

From the Theurgia Goetia:

"These Spirits are by nature Evil & very false & not to be trusted in Secrets but are excellent in driving away Spirits of Darkness from any that is haunted as houses, & to call forth Pamersiel or any of these his servants, make a circle in the form as is showed in the 1st. Book Goetia before going in the upper room of your house, or in a place that is Airy because these Spirits that are in this part are all Airy. You may call these Spirits into a Crystal Stone 4 inches Diameter" - Theurgia Goetia.

Do they have a direction? "Pamersiel is the first & chief Spirit ruling in the East under Canesiel" Yes of course they do. What about this Carnesiel's rank, does he have an earthly rank? "Carnesiel is the most chief & great Emperor ruling the East." There you go, he has an Earthly rank.

Now if we move to the Discoverie of Witchcrafte and there are quite a few spells which show how the crystal works for different types of spirits. This first spell is to conjure the spirit of the 'fairie' Sybylia. But first we are informed we need to get a go between. You set out to go and conjure a dead person who had killed himself (thus wouldn't be in heaven, according to the beliefs at the time, or simply they felt had sinned and was fair game.)

"begin the conjuration as followeth, and the spirit will appeare to you in the christall stone, in a faire forme of a child of twelve yeares of age. And when he is in, feele the stone, and it will be hot; and feare nothing, for he or shee will shew manie delusions, to drive you from your worke. Feare God, but feare him not. This is to constraine him, as followeth." you then give the constraint to force him into the crystal.

"doo appeare to me and to my fellow visiblie, immediatlie in this christall stone, and in a faire forme and shape of a child of twelve yeares of age, and that thou alter not thy shape" Yes his form is in the conjuration so you are actually telling him to appear a certain way. No surprise there.

It then continues:

"And when he is appeared in the christall stone, as is said before, bind him with this bond," So you can see that the crystal is being used for binding here, as there is an idea that he could possibly escape.

You make some chalk circles and set him out to go and fetch the fairie Sybylia which then comes in to the crystal instead. You bind her again into it with another bond.

Another from the Discoverie of Witchcrafte, by Reginald Scott is titled how to enclose a spirit in a crystal, which basically means to bind a spirit in to a crystal. This is a pretty interesting rite because you are summoning visibly manifested spirits without crystals, to force and bind a spirit into a crystal. Among other things it shows that the crystal again is being used as a form of binding and not to see spirits as you are calling two visibly without it in the first place. It also shows how much spirits deeply dislike entering crystals for obvious reasons. You put a spirit in a triangle then you can force him to tell you the truth, you put a spirit in a crystal and you can force him to stay inside it as your prisoner and do whatever you wish like show you buried treasure.

You then summon some infernal Kings, yes Kings, from the North. The circle is complex but we are not discussing the exact rite just what it entails which is shown here "That done, they will call a certeine spirit, whom they will command to enter into the centre of the circled or round christall. Then put the christall betweene the two circles, and thou shalt see the christall made blacke." and followed up of course with "Then command them to command the spirit in the christall, not to depart out of the stone, till thou give him licence." So again the crystal is for binding.

In a third example in the Discoverie a spirit is again called, told to take the form of a twelve year old boy, and bound as soon as he is in it. Go figure!

In Chapter Seventeen again you summon a ghost who has to put his hand on a book, (physical) and then swear that he will attend a crystal or mirror or anything else like it to aid the magician whenever he calls in the future. You then bind him to the crystal he will come in from then on.

Dr John Dee (1527-1608) is probably the most famous occultists who used crystals for the purpose of visions, aided by Edward Kelly. Dr Dee was not just another magician, he actually became Queen Elizabeth I scientific adviser. She was in fact a little mesmerized by him at first.

Edward Kelly his assistant in this, unfortunately was likely nothing more than con man of dubious background. Nonetheless he pretty much always seemed to see visions in these crystals (insert skepticism) which Dee found very useful. The spirits in fact ended up giving them what could be considered an entirely new form of magic through the crystal referred to usually as Enochian.

Of course Kelley also told Dee that the Angel Uriel wanted them to share their wives with one another (not very angelic) which Dee foolishly did, so really what grounding does this new Enochian magic have in reality? Certainly I have tried to leave it out of this book for the most part being late and not really a source text of some of the other works, but I think I would skim over it purely for its questionable nature anyway.

Note however that Uriel was supposed to have handed him a crystal to see spirits and visions inside in the first place. (Colin Wilson. The Occult: A History. Random House, 1971, p 273-4) So that is him actually taking something from a spirit as is suggested for example in the Little Book of Black Venus with the treasure.

Dream invocations are rarely mentioned in the early grimoires, but certainly they do pop up. In the Key of Solomon for example there is often a dream spell for taking a lover in a dream, there is also a Moon pentacle which is used for being taught about herbs while you sleep. Note that dream invocations are not methods of binding. They are not something extra you are trying to do to gain more control over a spirit and so unlike crystals shouldn't be that difficult to achieve.

Funnily enough through experience I can tell you that the rule of how they appear in the dream follows the same rules as when they appear outside of it, by which I mean their appearance is still influenced by the astrology at the time (of the dream, not the original ceremony), which is handy of course as they will come when it is easier for them to take that form and thus it is easier for them to appear to you.

They are in a way what crystals have been made out to be: the easier method of seeing a spirit.

CHAPTER NINE
The Missing Factor for Visible Spirits

Many people ask me what is the key to visibly seeing a spirit. Of course there are many methods but not really a key. Some people attempt to bribe the spirit to appear, some people tend to try and befriend the spirit, some people try and command the spirit but it is better to allow it to take it's own form or not be too specific if you don't understand the mechanics of how they appear. A good example of this is perhaps a spirit which can be called at a certain time of year. It may be that the Sun in a specific sign is the defining point of its manifestation to that body so calling it outside of that time may make it much harder and in some cases impossible to take the form you expect. Again if a time to call is unmentioned it may be worth thinking about if one exists anyway if the spirit is always said to appear a certain way. Perhaps he is stationed specifically in a place that holds that form.

There are numerous methods of causing a spirit to take visible appearance in the grimoires, from candles which light up invisible spirits, to pentacles such as in the Key of Solomon, or the pentacles of the Earth in the Discoverie of Witchcrafte by Reginald Scott. Obviously having as many of these as possible is going to aid you. There are also spirits which you can evoke in various grimoires to aid you make others spirits appear or obey, but pentacles and the like shouldn't be your main focus.

Placement is important. Spirits generally don't like coming in to houses. Houses are Saturn ruled and generally have some familiar spirits setting up residence there straight away, so you are calling them to a place where they are having to come into a Saturn spirit's residence which they aren't too keen on. Most spirits like being outside. If you've ever been out of your body and had to move through something physical you will know it is also a horrible feeling, the phrase 'personal space' is relevant here in it's literal meaning as you do literally feel something is inside you as you pass through it although you don't physically feel it. So if you are going to do it inside a place, then leave a way in and out for them, strangely they tend to use the same methods as people. If there is a door they will usually come through the door if it is relevant to their direction so leave it open.

Going outside to a place which is suitable to the instructions given or to the spirits themselves is best. So for example rivers are good for Moon spirits as they are to do with water. In most cases you are to go to an area where people cannot see, as the spirits do not like to appear and other people have not earned the right to see them like you have. If you leave in loopholes in your ceremony like other people around then you can rest assured they will jump through them and you won't see them. I understand a lot of people modernly say that only the magician can see the spirit or that each person will see a spirit differently but that is pure rubbish. When they appear they appear as they are and to everyone the same that is present hence you are to do it away from prying eyes. It may be the case that during visions rather than manifestation only a single person can see them but we have no real source to know one way or another.

Rules of numbers are very important for spirit manifestation too, if it says make a circle nine feet then make it nine feet.

Also attend your area beforehand and make sure everything will run smoothly for the ritual. For example when a grimoire says go to an area first and clean it up before you use it like in the Key of Solomon use this to remove any troublesome stones and branches from the vicinity of where you are going to engrave your circle and do actually engrave the circle.

If you are following something else or another tradition then use their methods but again it is always good to visit the area beforehand and make sure everything is right for when you wish to do the ceremony. a kind of sympathetic familiarity with the place is a good idea, a link to the place and to you.

In the Ceremonial Magician view prayer is important as you are praying for the power to use God's name to have control of the spirits to carry out whatever you have asked God for you to have. So prayer is incredibly important and not to be skipped. Witches often feel they don't need to do this but actually they had their own traditional prayers too. For example they obeyed the fasting and the purity rule often for nine days, where instead the ninth day would be the day of the ritual unlike the tenth, they also prayed to the spirit everyday for seven days. Witchcraft was a variable though and different areas may have had different rites but it was usually still quite ceremonial.

In short there is no real quick easy 5 steps to visibly seeing spirits, but there are some pointers that you can adhere to.

Know who you are calling:

What they are supposed to look like, what time of the year they are supposed to be called etc.

Plan your ritual in advance:

A good time for planning is the new moon, but not for performing magic. Prepare everything you need then unless you are following rules otherwise stated and try not to deviate from decisions you make then. Make sure the area is suitable.

Know the Ascendant:

You are looking specifically at the sign that is ascending. There are many free astrology programs but to put it simply, if the Sun is in Libra, then Libra will ascend with the Sun and the same if it was with any other sign. The signs run in this order Aries, Taurus, Gemini, Cancer, Leo, Virgo, Libra, Scorpio, Sagittarius, Capricorn, Aquarius, Pisces and all will ascend once during a day. If a spirit often appears with a lion's head it will probably be easier called with the Sun in Leo or Leo ascending.

Follow the rules:

Follow the rules of whatever you book you are using to the letter. Any short cuts will be taken advantage of if the spirit does not want to appear. Coincidentally watch out for silly spells, for example "say X five times and spirit F will appear." Things aren't that simple. A lot of these simple spells descended from things much more complex. Traditional Witches for example didn't just do a ceremony like the Wiccans do now, they often had rhymes for gathering the things they needed. Often these basic things like the usual 9 day of purity before a ceremony is simply not stated because it was expected that you should already know it.

Give the spirit space to appear:

A spirit won't always appear where you want him to, if you can get him to appear happily in the triangle you are a better magician than I am. I am guessing there is an unwritten rule that they are following and you have to be pretty powerful to break it and get them to appear in the right spot straight away, especially if it is somewhere that you want to bind them, a crystal, triangle, brass vessel etc. So allow a lot of room for the spirit to manifest. 12 feet in all directions is pretty good and know that they will come from the direction they come from. I could write out a vary complex system which explains why the same spirits are recorded coming from set directions yet differ from grimoire to one another, but really you don't need it. Face where it tells you and expect them to turn up wherever they do then try and get them into the triangle or whatever binding method you are using if you feel that is required.

Time limit is a huge factor:

Possibly one of the reasons I have had success is I had no concept of banishing spirits when I first started so

I don't. I call them and then wait for them to turn up. sometimes they can be 12 hours late but that is pretty extreme. I have even had them turn up the same day but exactly a week later when it was easier for them to come. So don't summon them for 5 minutes and then send them away without them actually turning up because by doing this you are stopping them from turning up at all. Banishing in the grimoires is generally following the appearance of a spirit. It's quite plausible you have done something wrong and not got the power to pull it right from where it is and that it will come to you when it does, it's unlikely you have done everything right and they just didn't turn up. So if you think you have performed everything correctly as is written down in whatever you are following, and they haven't turned up, wait for them and make sure they turn up before you tell them they are released from your call. I suppose for other types of magic banishing may be more or less important but it's still a good idea to take this in mind.

Religion:

This is a controversial one to address, but the fact is many of the grimoires were Christian or Jewish in religion and some even had curses that if you would use it for bad purposes or did not follow God then it would not work. If you believe in the grimoires, then you must also believe in these curses. Also just because they are not stated in all grimoires does not mean that they weren't put on them. The grimoires rely on God's power of a spirit and you earning the right to use his name to command them through the purity etc. If you are an avid hater of that particular God, then I'm afraid you aren't likely to get very far with him allowing you control.

CHAPTER TEN
Final thoughts

Ignoring my own experiences and just looking at the grimoires themselves still there are various points we can take from this.

A spirit has physical attributes like the ability to crush a person, and is the image as it is referred to, so it is not a vision.

Also that his form is changeable, so he is not a solid creature in the terms that we are either at least not until he takes a form.

Coincidentally he can move through things also if he wishes to, as he gets into the crystal in the first place so solidity is not a set attribute of theirs like it ours, and through attacking things invisibly we know that it does not have to become visible to have some physical form. Again this is partly though not completely backed by the Key of Knowledge's reference to the candle 'lighting up' the spirit.

A spirit is not omnipresent, you call it from where it is specifically to the circle.

Visible & Physical Spirit Manifestation of Spirits

A look from inside the Grimoires

There is a system that they appear to follow for their manifestation which is largely astrological, and that system may be vital in some success and failures and even suggest stations of spirits, though as many spirits have appeared a number of ways, some are clearly more flexible with this. We should say that there are certainly different types or classes of spirits through this alone.

These are all things discussed that are worth considering in the future when looking at the truth behind visible and physical manifestations of spirits and I hope that this book has enriched your stance on visible appearance of spirits in the grimoires, how it works according to the grimoires and how perhaps you can take information of circumstance to aid you have the physical appearance of a spirit in whatever path you follow yourself.

Some tips for reference on the features of ascendants that I have found:

Aries: ram, goat, dark hair, dark eyes, body builder frame, soldier, gladiator, sometimes dark skin or tanned skin, armed with sword.

Taurus: short, stocky, wide necks, dark hair and eyes, attractive, wide jaw, hoofed animal, horned animal, bull.

Gemini: Twins, two headed, brothers, blonde hair, thin, intelligent.

Cancer: Average build, blue eyed, rain, moon.

Leo: Jungle, rainforest, lions, cats, red hair, sometimes curly hair, green or blue eyed, medication, sun.

Virgo: Skeptical, faithless, commandeering, ill, dark hair, large forehead, small pointed chin, can be overweight especially in the belly.

Libra: Blonde hair, blue eyes, good looking, sometimes well built, relationship orientated, often wear white, scales, court, sword.

Scorpio: Dark hair and dark eyes, prominent nose, blunt in reply, Scorpios, black in skin, knight, martyr, intelligence, sex, well built or very thin, tall, eagles, dragons, snakes.

Sagittarius: Cantaur, horses, black skin, bows and arrows, large hands and feet, hooves, long thick hair.

Capricorn: narrow chests, thin necks, small eyes, wrinkles, curled horns, hooves, black skin.

Aquarius: Fishes, rain, sea, defined in sex, squarish forehead.

Pisces: Fish often in pairs, deformity, over weight, fleshy, feet.

I wish you good luck in your endeavors.

References

Esotericarchives.com

A problem of Authorship: John Dee, Edward Kelley and the Angelic Conversations by R. Christopher Feldman

Max Heindel

www.ingramcontent.com/pod-product-compliance
Ingram Content Group UK Ltd.
Pitfield, Milton Keynes, MK11 3LW, UK
UKHW041838200726
13854UKWH00003BA/1209